Buses, Coaches, Trolleyb...
& Recollections 1968

Contents

Acknowledgments

A large number of the illustrations in this book are from the camera of Bob Gell. Without these views and the detailed notes on each slide, this book would not have been possible. My most sincere thanks to Bob — outstanding!

The PSV Circle Fleet Histories for the operators in this book and a No of issues of *Buses Illustrated* were vital sources of information.

© Henry Conn 2015
First published in 2015

British Library Cataloguing in Publication Data
A catalogue record for this book is available from the British Library.

ISBN 978 1 85794 450 1
Silver Link Publishing Ltd
The Trundle
Ringstead Road
Great Addington
Kettering
Northants NN14 4BW

Tel/Fax: 01536 330588
email: sales@nostalgiacollection.com
Website: www.nostalgiacollection.com

Printed and bound in Ceská Republika

About the author

My first recollections of public transport were early in 1958 in my home town of Aberdeen, travelling from our home in Mastrick to Union Street, then onwards by tram to Bridge of Dee. My interest in buses, trolleybuses and trams expanded to taking fleet numbers or registration numbers, and by the mid-1960s I had acquired a camera and began my collection. This interest continued through my family's moves from Aberdeen to Perth, Whitburn in West Lothian, Banbury, Swindon and Oxford by 1974.

My first job was with Customs & Excise, beginning in London with transfers to Oxford, Dover and Brighton. It was after I left Brighton that my enthusiasm for bus photography waned, and it never really returned apart from sporadic photography when I returned to Scotland in 1980. By this time I had left Customs & Excise and had returned to college in Cupar to study Agriculture. I met my future wife at this college and moved with her parents to Galloway, where I have lived very happily since 1983. To further my career I attended Aberdeen University to take a BSc Degree in Agriculture, and I successfully graduated in 1996. This led to me returning to the Civil Service with the Scottish Executive Rural Affairs Department, then through many changes to where I am now, working with Natural England as adviser to farmers on Environmental Schemes (three days a week from last July).

By 2010 I had a significant collection of transport views from the mid-1960s to the early 1980s. I met with Silver Link Publishing's editor Will Adams in Preston in early 2010 and was very kindly given the opportunity to write a volume on Buses, Trams and Trolleybuses in the Midlands. Since then I have continued to enjoy writing volumes on transport for Silver Link, this volume being my second in the 'Recollections' series looking at buses, trolleybuses and trams as well as significant events in a specific year.

Introduction

The year 1968 was the year of 'sex and drugs and rock'n'roll'; it was also the year of the assassinations of Martin Luther King and Bobby Kennedy, the Prague Spring, the Chicago convention, the Tet offensive in Vietnam and the anti-war movement, the student rebellion that paralysed France, civil rights, the beginning of the end for the Soviet Union, and the birth of the women's movement. It was the year when television's impact on global events first became apparent, and when simultaneously, in Paris, Prague, London and Berkeley, and all over the globe, uprisings spontaneously occurred.

The communication and technological breakthroughs in 1968 brought the whole world into closer focus and paved the way for the barrage of information with which we now live. I remember many of these events seeping into our lives from the streets, the schools, the radio and the nightly news, but never considered just how much upheaval was packed into one amazing year. This was a watershed year – we saw TV from space, and US sprinters Tommie Smith and John Carlos raised black-gloved fists in protest during the medals ceremony at the Olympic Games in Mexico City. Within this volume are further facts and anecdotes from a tumultuous year.

Once again the pictures take us on a journey from north to south, then from Wales and the South West to end in Kent. Enjoy the nostalgia!

Frontispiece: **DOUGLAS, IoM** Douglas purchased five Mulliner-bodied Guy Otters new in late 1957. They were numbered 8 to 12 (WMN 484 to 488), and No 12 is seen working route 32 on 6 September 1968. Although bearing a resemblance to similar Guy buses for London Transport, the Douglas vehicles always carried the large destination indicators that earned them the nickname of 'Wolsey's camels', after the then General Manager at Douglas. These little buses were used on routes throughout Douglas, and could also often be seen on the out-of-town route to Port Soderick. They had a normal control design, like the cars of the day, with the engine in front; this meant that the driver could sit opposite the entrance. However, the drivers had a hard time with these 'camels', with very heavy steering and a back-to-front gear arrangement. Despite this, all five Douglas examples found further use when they were withdrawn in 1970. *Author's collection*

DOUGLAS, IoM This is Isle of Man Road Services No 20 (WMN 6), one of four Weymann-bodied Leyland PSUC1/1s new in 1957. The bus was re-seated to dual purpose in April 1963, and this view, taken on 6 September 1968, clearly shows the high-backed seating. No 20 was withdrawn from service June 1981 and was used for staff transport for a few months; it is now in preservation.

Cunningham's holiday camp on Victoria Road, Douglas, was one of the earliest in the British Isles (pre-dating Butlin's), opening around 1902. Initially there were only steps leading to the camp from the seafront, but from about 1919 they were replaced by a moving chairlift known as Cunningham's Camp Escalator, thought to have been built by J.T. Skillicorn of Onchan. In 1938 a second escalator was provided, both only working in the up direction and running within a wooden shelter. The escalator last functioned in 1968, after which it was closed off but not demolished. *Author's collection*

Photo	DESTINATIONS
1	ISLE OF MAN
2	ISLE OF MAN
3	LANCASTER
4	LANCASTER
5	LANCASTER
6	LANCASTER
7	LEEDS
8	LEEDS
9	LEEDS
10	LEEDS
11	LEEDS
12	LEEDS
13	BRADFORD
14	BRADFORD
15	BRADFORD
16	HALIFAX
17	HALIFAX
18	HALIFAX
19	HALIFAX
20	HALIFAX

LANCASTER The date is 11 August 1968, and standing in Lancaster bus station is No 175 (175 FTJ), one of three East Lancashire-bodied Leyland PSUC1/3s new to the city in September and October 1978. Two of the Tiger Cubs were withdrawn in September 1973, but No 175 was still in the Lancaster fleet when the amalgamation with Morecambe formed the Lancaster City Council Passenger Department, although it was not retained much longer thereafter.

1T57, the so-called 'Fifteen Guinea Special', was the last main-line passenger train to be hauled by steam locomotive power on British Railways on this day; a steam ban was introduced the following day. It was a special rail tour excursion organised for the occasion, travelling from Liverpool via Manchester to Carlisle and back, and was pulled by four different steam locomotives in turn during the four legs of the journey.

One of my favourite films was released in the UK three days before the view below was taken – The Graduate with Dustin Hoffman and Anne Bancroft.

LANCASTER Fifteen Northern Counties-bodied Leyland PDR1/2 were purchased new by Ribble in May and June 1967, and this is No 1953 (ECK 953E) at Lancaster bus station on 11 August 1968.

LANCASTER On the same day and in the same location, this is No 204 (KTJ 204C), an East Lancashire-bodied Leyland PD2/37 new in 1965.

On this day the Beatles launched their Apple Records label.

LANCASTER When 30-foot double-deckers became legal in the UK in 1956, Ribble took the plunge in a big way by placing an order for 105 Leyland PD3/4s with Burlingham bodywork. These buses began to enter service in late 1957 and caused quite a stir with their unusual full fronts and front entrances. They were spread widely around the company operating area, but large numbers were based in Liverpool and Carlisle, where their large capacity was useful on urban services. Subsequently, Ribble purchased a large batch of similar buses, but this time with Metro-Cammell bodywork and semi-automatic gearboxes. This is the first Burlingham-bodied Leyland PD3/4, No 1501 (KCK 847) working towards Heysham on 7 April 1968. *Author's collection*

On this day, very sadly, racing driver Jim Clark was killed at Hockenheim.

LEEDS In 1950 Leeds Corporation took delivery of 25 Roe-bodied AEC Regent IIIs, Nos 601 to 625 (NUB 601 to 625), and representing this batch at Leeds bus station on a wet and gloomy 20 March 1968 is No 610 (NUB 610). This bus would remain in the fleet until it was sold for scrap in June 1969.

On 29 March the Victoria Hall in Leeds played host to the Bee Gees.

LEEDS A total of 55 Roe-bodied AEC Regent Vs were purchased new by Leeds Corporation in 1957, and one of these, working route 68 to Foundry Lane, also on 20 March 1968, is No 840 (XUM 840).

A couple of weeks earlier Radio Caroline had gone off the air at 5.20am, with no closing announcement. Both Caroline ships were forced to stop broadcasting and were towed away to the port of Amsterdam due to major debts.

LEEDS Daimler CVG6LX30 Roe H39/31Fs Nos 572-576 (572 to 576 CNW) were the first front-entrance double-deckers in the fleet, and were purchased in 1962 specifically for the Leeds to Bradford service; this was jointly operated with Bradford Corporation, and the latter mainly used front-entrance vehicles. Standing at Leeds bus station on 20 March 1968 working the Bradford service is No 576 (576 CNW).

In March 1963 a gallon of petrol cost 5s 5d, and on the day this view was taken footballer Paul Merson was born in Harlesden, London.

Right: **LEEDS** Kippax Motors had four Leyland PD3s, a Leyland PD2 and two Daimler CVD6 buses when Wallace Arnold sold the company, together with the Farsley Motor Company, to Leeds Corporation on 31 March 1968. This is DUG 166C at Leeds bus station on that same March day; note the advert for Wallace Arnold, at that time still the owners of Kippax Motors.

Below: **LEEDS** This view of No 66 (MNW 166F), a Metro-Cammell-Weymann-bodied AEC Swift, was taken at The Headrow, also on 20 March. Being driven with Warwickshire trade plates and without a fleet name, it is fairly certain that this bus has been captured on the day of its delivery to Leeds Corporation.

At the time this view was taken singer/songwriter Cat Stevens was in hospital with tuberculosis, and would remain hospitalised for three months.

Right: **LEEDS** This view of Leeds Corporation's No 256 (5256 NW), a Roe-bodied Leyland PD3/5 new in 1959, was taken on 27 September. *Author's collection*

On this day the American musical **Hair** *opened in London following the removal of theatre censorship.*

BRADFORD Working route 7 on 20 March 1968 is Bradford No 737 (DKY 737). New in March 1946 with Roe bodywork, No 737 received a new East Lancashire body in December 1959. Originally fitted with a Metro-Vick 85hp motor, it was fitted with an EEC 120hp motor from a Notts Derby BUT 9611T. No 737 was withdrawn in 1972 and stored at Thornbury Depot for preservation.

A few days before this view was taken the Elite Cinema in Toller Road, Bradford, reopened as the Star Bingo Club.

BRADFORD A total of ten Karrier W chassis were purchased from South Wales in December 1952 and January 1953; they had been new to Llanelly & District Traction in 1945 and 1946. This is No 776 (CBX 531) at Thornbury Depot, also on 20 March. It had received a new East Lancashire body in February 1956 and entered service in the same month, remaining in the fleet until 1971, when it was sold for scrap. Thornbury Depot was closed for trolleybuses on 31 July 1971 and to buses on 27 March 1977.

*Films released in March 1968 were **Romeo and Juliet**, **Madigan** and **Guess Who's Coming to Dinner**.*

BRADFORD In November 1950 Bradford took delivery of three Weymann-bodied BUT 9611Ts, Nos 752, 753 and 755 (FKU 752, 753 and 755). This is No 753, heading for Thornbury Depot on 20 March 1968; it was to survive until late 1970, when it was sold for scrap. The bus whose rear end appears in the background is No 174 (2174 KW), a Metro-Cammell-bodied AEC Regent V new in 1963.

Right: **HALIFAX** The only new rear-engine double-deck bus in the Hebble fleet was No 351 (DJX 351D), a Northern Counties-bodied Daimler CRG6LX new in July 1966; it is seen at Halifax bus station on 20 March 1968. No 351 passed to Yorkshire Woollen in April 1971, then to Halifax Joint Omnibus Committee in August of that year, to Calderdale Joint Omnibus Committee in September, and finally to West Yorkshire Passenger Transport Executive in April 1974. After preservation, the bus was sold for export to the USA.

On this day the No 1 single in the UK was The Legend of Xanadu by Dave, Dee, Dozy, Beaky, Mick and Tich.

Left: **HALIFAX** A Dennis Loline demonstrator with Northern Counties bodywork, a Gardner 6LX engine and a four-speed semi-automatic gearbox visited Halifax in 1964. Further visits were arranged, and as a result Halifax ordered five Northern Counties Dennis Loline IIIs with five-speed gearboxes, Nos 300 to 304 (FCP 300E to 304E), delivered in 1967. They were fitted with high-backed seats and air suspension at the rear, and were lively performers. Unfortunately, mechanical problems arose soon after entry into service, the main one being a complicated and congested transmission area. After only four years in service Halifax Corporation decided to dispose of the buses and they were acquired by West Riding to replace the Wulfrunians. The Lolines lasted for a further seven years with West Riding, then all five were sold for scrap in 1978. At Halifax bus station on 20 March 1968 is No 304 (FCP 304E).

HALIFAX During June 1967 Halifax took delivery of three Willowbrook-bodied Daimler SRG6LXs, Nos 106 to 108 (FJX 506E to 508E). Working a local town service to Norton Tower at Halifax bus station on that same day in March is No 106 (FJX 506E). As West Yorkshire Passenger Transport Executive No 3106, this bus was the last of the Halifax SRG6LXs to be withdrawn form service, on 9 January 1991.

Just over two weeks after the date of this view, the film 2001: A Space Odyssey was premiered in Washington, DC.

Below left: **HALIFAX** Todmorden Joint Omnibus Committee was a staunch devotee of the Leyland marque, and for a period its fleet consisted solely of 38 PD2s dating from between 1947 and 1951. This is Todmorden's No 27 (KWX 19), an all-Leyland PD2/12 new in 1951; it was one of the last double-deckers purchased by Todmorden. Indeed, the committee purchased no new buses for the next decade, switching to Leyland Leopards in 1961. This view was taken in Halifax on 20 March 1968.

Just 10 days after this picture was taken Celine Dion was born in Quebec, Canada.

Below: **HALIFAX** This is Todmorden No 18 (HWY 36), an all-Leyland PD2/1 new in 1950. Note the advertisement for Webster's Green Label, which when this view was taken was brewed at the Fountain Head Brewery of Samuel Webster & Sons Ltd at Ovenden Wood. This view dates from 24 September 1968 and the Hillman Hunter (Minx) behind No 18 has been on the road for a very short time. The car's image was boosted when a Hunter driven by Andrew Cowan won the London to Sydney Marathon Rally in this year. *Author's collection*

TODMORDEN Entering Todmorden Market Ground (bus station) on 3 September 1968 is all-Leyland PD2/1 No 25 (KWX 18). The Todmorden Viaduct, with its nine arches, was built in 1840 by Robert Stephenson to carry the Manchester to Leeds railway over Burnley Road. The car on the left heading in the opposite direction is a Ford Zodiac from 1966, which was the final year of production of this marque. *Author's collection*

Keith Emerson of Nice and Emerson, Lake & Palmer was born in Todmorden. Nice were banned from playing at London's Royal Albert Hall for burning an American flag on stage on 26 June 1968.

WAKEFIELD The Wulfrunian could be tricky to drive in slippery or icy conditions, especially when travelling uphill, and all that unladen weight at the front end resulted in accelerated wear on critical suspension and steering components such as the king pins and shock absorbers. Wulfrunians also suffered from abnormal front tyre wear, again caused by weight balance deficiencies. This spurred operators to remove the front two rows of seats on the upper deck, reducing the capacity by eight passengers, in an attempt to preserve the life of the components. This is West Riding's Roe-bodied Guy Wulfrunian No 972 (WHL 972), new in October 1963, at Wakefield bus station on 20 March 1968.

WAKEFIELD Look at the angle of the front wheel on Guy Wulfrunian No 873 (SHL 873), new in January 1963! The bus is in the red and cream tram route livery for services from Leeds to Kettlethorpe and Rothwell. This view was taken on 8 January 1968. *Author's collection*

On this day Harold Wilson endorsed the 'I'm Backing Britain' campaign for working an additional half-hour each day without pay!

CASTLEFORD The Wulfrunian was a very advanced bus and a very bold design; however, the manufacturer was nearly bankrupt and development of the bus was therefore seriously curtailed. In service its poor performance established a reputation that it was never able to shake off, and a traditional British bus industry would not buy into it. The ride quality, however, was second to none, and it provided new standards of passenger comfort ahead of its time. The last Wulfrunian appeared at the closure of the Bradford trolleybus system and the entire fleet was disposed of in just 12 years, some of the buses being a mere four years old when they went for scrap. This is No 867 (SHL 867), a Roe-bodied Guy Wulfrunian new in 1960; when photographed on 6 September 1968 it was into its eighth year of service. *Author's collection*

CASTLEFORD Working a Castleford local service to Ferry Fryston on 4 September 1968 is No 1005, (BHL 356C), one of a batch of 30 Roe-bodied Guy Wulfrunians new in January 1965. In the background is one of the 1957 Roe-bodied Guy Arab IVs, No 829 (KHL 829), which had a longer than normal service life due to the early withdrawal of the Wulfrunians. *Author's collection*

Four days after the date of this view Virginia Wade beat Billie Jean King at the US Open; she is the only British woman in history to have won titles at all four Grand Slam tournaments.

1968
No 1 Records

January
Georgie Fame — *The Ballad of Bonnie and Clyde*
Love Affair — *Everlasting Love*

February
Manfred Mann — *Mighty Quinn*
Esther and Abi Ofarim — *Cinderella Rockafella*

March
Dave Dee, Dozy, Beaky, Mick and Tich
— *The Legend of Xanadu*
Beatles — *Lady Madonna*

April
Cliff Richard — *Congratulations*
Louis Armstrong — *What a Wonderful World/Cabaret*

May
Gary Puckett and the Union Gap — *Young Girl*

June
Rolling Stones — *Jumpin' Jack Flash*

July
Equals — *Baby Come Back*
Des O'Connor — *I Pretend*
Tommy James and the Shondells — *Mony Mony*

August
Crazy World of Arthur Brown — *Fire*
Beach Boys — *Do It Again*

September
Bee Gees — *I've Gotta Get a Message to You*
Beatles — *Hey Jude*
Mary Hopkin — *Those Were The Days*

November
Joe Cocker — *With a Little Help from my Friends*
Hugo Montenegro and his Orchestra
— *The Good, The Bad and The Ugly*

December
Scaffold — *Lily the Pink*

CASTLEFORD Standing in Castleford Depot on 4 September 1968 are Nos A15 and A14 (BHL 676 and 684), all-Leyland PD2/1s new in 1948, in their role as driver trainers. *Author's collection*

Hey Jude by the Beatles was released on 30 August and the single had a 16-week run on the British charts from 7 September, claiming No 1 a week later.

MIRFIELD

Photographed on 13 October 1968, this is KTD 551C, a Sheffield-designed Park Royal-bodied Leyland PDR1/1 new as a demonstrator in 1965. It was purchased by Joseph Wood & Son of Mirfield and ran on the Mirfield to Dewsbury service, which was joint with J. J. Longstaff and Yorkshire Woollen District. This bus has a claim to fame as it was driven by Prince Philip at Leyland Motors in July 1966 for a mile on the test track, and the passengers included Sir Donald Stokes and Sir William Black, who were Managing Director and Chairman of Leyland Motors. The lovely red car in the background is a Volvo P1800, a model that will be remembered by many as Simon Templar's car in the early 1960s TV series *The Saint*. *Author's collection*

On the day of this photograph the rebuilt Euston railway station opened.

PONTEFRACT Guy launched the all-new Wulfrunian in 1958, featuring air suspension, independent on the front axle, and Dunlop-developed disc brakes. A drop rear axle was fitted to provide a lower chassis so that low bridges could be passed under, and the all-new Gardner 6LX 10.5-litre diesel was mounted at the front. The chassis was tough and substantial, like Guy products that came before it, but the combined weight of the driveline and complicated independent front suspension sub-frame gave the bus a massive weight bias over the front axle. Standing in Pontefract bus station on 20 March 1968 is Roe-bodied Guy Wulfrunian No 865 (SHL 865), new to West Riding in December 1960.

PONTEFRACT These two South Yorkshire buses are standing in the town's bus station on the same day. On the left is No 61 (GWY 630), a Burlingham-bodied Albion CX13 new in December 1947; this was the first coach to be purchased by South Yorkshire after the end of the Second World War. No 61 received the 1950 coach body from JWT 112 in 1958. In the centre is No 75 (KWY 223), an all-Leyland PD2/12 new in November 1951.

HUDDERSFIELD Working the cross-town Huddersfield trolleybus service 71 from Waterloo to Lindley on 20 March 1968 is East Lancashire-bodied BUT 9641T No 629 (KVH 229). This much-loved trolleybus system would cease to operate within four months. Wearing the excellent streamlined livery behind No 629 is No 464 (KVH 464D), an East Lancashire-bodied Daimler CVG6LX new in 1966.

CHESTER The last ECW-bodied Bristol LL6Bs were delivered to Crosville during 1952, numbered KW 274 to 293 (NFM 30 to 49). In May 1958 they were renumbered SLB 270 to 293, and this view of No SLB 290 (NFM 46) was taken in Chester on 10 October 1968; this would be one of the last LL6Bs in the Crosville fleet, remaining until mid-1970. No 290 spent much of its final days working from Chester operating routes C6 and C7, Chester to Ellesmere Port via the villages of Stoak and Stannage, together with a short working in Ellesmere Port. *Author's collection*

At this time in 1968 the M1 motorway was completed when the final 35-mile section between Rotherham and Leeds opened.

BIRKENHEAD A total of 30 Bristol ECW 60-seat FSF Lodekkas were delivered to Crosville between October 1961 and June 1962. Whereas the FLF Lodekka was a 30-foot-long forward-entrance 70-seater, the FSF was 27 feet long with a forward entrance and 60 seats. Although not foreseen at the time, these proved to be Crosville's only FSFs. The first five, Nos DFB 54 to 58 (864 to 868 VFM), had Bristol BVW engines and were model FSF6B. The other 25 had Gardner 6LW engines and were model FSF6G. All 30 had four-speed crash gearboxes. At least six of the FSF6Gs were allocated to Liverpool's Edge Lane depot. Warrington depot had further examples, which appeared on a daily basis on its three routes to Liverpool, the H1, H2 and H5. In the foreground here at Rock Ferry Depot on 30 September 1968 is No DFB 55 (865 VFM), which passed to a dealer for scrap in April 1976. *Author's collection*

BIRKENHEAD Standing in Rock Ferry Depot on the same day is No DFB 88 (898 VFM), an ECW-bodied Bristol FLF6B new in October 1961. This FLF was fitted with a Cave-Brown-Cave heating system, fluorescent lighting and illuminated offside advertisement panels. Compare the FLF to the Bristol LD6G No DLG 796 (XFM 207) in the right background, which was new in June 1956. The latter passed to Cheshire County Council as a play-bus and remained so until July 1980, outlasting the FLF, which went to a dealer in June 1977. The main routes operated by Rock Ferry were those from Birkenhead Woodside to Chester. The C1 was the direct route, while the C3 and C4 operated via Ellesmere Port, and together the three routes provided a frequent service along the New Chester Road. There were also short journeys on the C3 around Ellesmere Port, providing a kind of town service. There was also the C2, which was an occasional service to Chester Zoo. Rock Ferry also operated many other routes to the southern end of the Wirral and into North Wales, which were numbered in the 'F' series. *Author's collection*

Mary Hopkin topped the UK charts for 6 weeks from 24 September with **Those Were the Days.**

BIRKENHEAD Working route F27 between Birkenhead Woodside and Meols via Arrowe Park and Caldy in the Wirral on 10 December 1968 is No CMG 467 (2172 FM), an ECW-bodied Bristol MW6G new in March 1963. It was fitted with Cave-Brown-Cave heating, was 31 feet long, and had its original curved roof lights replaced by fibreglass panels in 1967. This bus was exported to the Irish Republic in December 1976. The car in the background is a Volvo P120. *Author's collection*

The average annual wage in 1968 was just under £1,489.

RHYL The first ECW-bodied Bristol RELH6Gs were delivered to Crosville in January 1964. The next two, new in June of that year, were Nos CRG 524 and 525 (7285 and 7286 FM), and on tour in Rhyl on 13 July 1968 is No CRG 524. Both coaches survived with Crosville until mid-1980. *Author's collection*

The Equals' single Baby Come Back was No 1 on this day, and Gary Player won the 97th British Open at Carnoustie, Scotland.

MATLOCK During 1968 North Western took delivery of 40 Marshall-bodied Bristol RESL6Gs, Nos 270 to 309 (KJA 270F to 309F). Standing in Matlock bus station on 10 August 1968 is the nearly new No 289 (KJA 289F); this bus passed to the South East Lancashire Passenger Transport Executive in January 1972, and subsequently to the Greater Manchester Passenger Transport Executive on 1 April 1974, with the fleet number 1619.

Just about to be released in British cinemas were The Green Berets with John Wayne and The Good, The Bad and The Ugly with Clint Eastwood.

ILKESTON The final batch of Eastern Coachwork-bodied Bristol LS6Gs for Midland General arrived during 1956. They all had dual-purpose bodywork and were numbered 242 to 253 (956 to 967 ARA). This view of No 251 (965 ARA) was taken in Ilkeston on 6 February 1968; it was acquired by Cumberland during October 1971, which gave it the fleet number 220. Overtaking the bus is a Hillman Imp.

On this day the 1968 Winter Olympics opened in Grenoble, France.

THE C8 ALSO WENT TO SWINGATE (WHITE LION PUB)
D. Pratt /9. 8·2015/

NOTTINGHAM

This is Nottingham City Transport's No 45 (45 ATO), the last numerically of 44 Metro-Cammell-Weymann-bodied Leyland PD2/40s new between February 1958 and March 1959; it is working route 40 to Wilford Road in King Edward Street on 30 June 1968. This bus would later become a training vehicle between July 1976 and June 1977 before being sold for scrap.

Small Faces with Lazy Sunday topped the singles chart at the end of June 1968.

Right: **NOTTINGHAM** The distinctive Nottingham design for rear-engine buses was first introduced at the 1964 Commercial Motor Show, and by the end of 1980 446 examples had been produced. Seen at the same location on the same day, and representing an early example of the Nottingham design, is No 427 (DAU 427C), a Metro-Cammell-Weymann-bodied Leyland PDR1/2 new in April 1965. It later passed to Hutchings & Cornelius in January 1979, then a few months later to Tor Coaches of Street.

One of my favourite songs was released in June 1968, Born to be Wild by Steppenwolf. The song would become very popular the following year when it featured in the film Easy Rider.

Below: **NOTTINGHAM** Taking on passengers for a journey to London at Huntingdon Street bus station on 29 May 1968 is Trent No 101 (HRC 101C), a Y Type with Alexander coach bodywork new in 1965. In the background is Lancashire United No 152 (DTF 582B), a Plaxton dual-purpose-bodied Leyland PSU3/3R new in May 1964.

A few hours after this view was taken, Manchester United defeated Benfica 4-1 after extra time to become the first English winners of the European Cup.

NOTTINGHAM An unusual bus to arrive from Great Yarmouth at Huntingdon Street on the same day is brand-new Eastern Counties ECW bus-bodied Bristol RELL6G No RL677 (PPW 677F) – this service was normally operated by a coach.

A little over a month after this view was taken the first episode of Dad's Army was broadcast.

Left: **NOTTINGHAM** Turning into Huntingdon Street bus station on the same day is East Yorkshire No 682 (6682 KH), a Leyland PSUC1/2 with a Metro-Cammell Weymann dual-purpose body, new in August 1960. This bus was painted in the cream and light blue coach livery from new, and was converted for one-person operation in September 1964. It passed to United Counties in May 1972 and was then acquired by McAlpine in October 1972, remaining with that contractor until May 1976. Note the adverts for tyres – the Michelin ZX tyre was first made in 1968.

Above: **NOTTINGHAM** In July 1953 Lincolnshire took delivery of a new ECW coach-bodied Bristol LS6B No 988 (KBE 179); this was exchanged with an ECW coach-bodied Bristol LS6G from Southern Vectis, JDL 756, in October 1953, which became Lincolnshire's No 2007. JDL 756 is seen here in Huntingdon Street bus station, also on 29 May 1968; it was purchased for spares by Western National of Exeter in November 1972.

Bristol F.L.F. on 138 route
D Smith
(16.8.2015)

NOTTINGHAM The fleet of West Bridgford Urban District Council passed to Nottingham City Transport on the night of 28/29 September 1968. Service 21 was West Bridgford's premier route, and was always worked with the newest buses – it had not been worked by AEC Regent IIIs for many years. This view in Trent Street on 30 September 1968 is therefore rare, showing former West Bridgford No 3 (HNN 773) on the 21 route; this Park Royal-bodied Regent III was by now No 169 in the Nottingham fleet. It did not last long, however, and was sold for scrap in June 1969.

Below left: **NOTTINGHAM** West Bridgford took delivery of three Park Royal-bodied AEC Regent Vs in November and December 1955, numbered 28 to 30 (TRR 951 to 953). They were the first Regent Vs to be purchased new by West Bridgford, and No 28, the first delivered, is working route 15A in Carrington Street on 25 September 1968. This bus became No 274 in the Nottingham fleet and passed to a Barnsley dealer for scrap in May 1970. The passing car is a new Vauxhall Viva.

On this day actor Will Smith was born in West Philadelphia, Pennsylvania.

Below: **NOTTINGHAM** Newly arrived at Barton's Chilwell Depot at the beginning of June 1968 is 211 JUS, a Park Royal-bodied AEC Renown new in 1963. This bus and 212 JUS were new to Smiths of Barrhead in Scotland; Barton purchased both and they were based at the Ilkeston Garage on Manor Road, mainly used on routes 52 and 53 from Ilkeston to Kirk Hallam Estate. No 1102 (RRY 464) is a Plaxton-bodied Bedford SBG new to Mason & Sons Limited of Leicester in May 1957; this fleet was acquired in April 1967, and No 1102 was retained in the Barton fleet for a short time until sold to the West Bridgford Scouts in January 1969.

Above: **NOTTINGHAM** At Huntingdon Street bus station on 29 May 1968 is Barton No 719 (RAL 43), a Plaxton-bodied Leyland BTS/1 new in 1953.

In May 1968 the price of a pint of milk varied between 11d and 1s 2d. Four days before the date of this view the Rolling Stones released Jumpin' Jack Flash.

Left: **NOTTINGHAM** The last two AEC Regent Vs new to West Bridgford were Nos 39 and 40 (639 and 640 NVO). At St Peter's Gate on 25 September 1968 is No 39 (639 NVO), which had Park Royal bodywork and was new in January 1964. After withdrawal by Nottingham in 1974, it passed to the London Borough of Waltham Forest, where it remained until August 1978; by April 1979 it was noted at Bicester Gliding School. The West Bridgford bus in the background is No 43 (NAL 543F), one of three East Lancashire-bodied AEC Swifts new in September 1967; all three would later pass to Heyfordian Travel Limited in 1976, remaining with that company until October 1979.

On this night the 801st episode of Coronation Street was broadcast.

On 4 April 1968 Dr Martin Luther King was shot dead by a sniper in Memphis. On 8 June, a week after this view was taken, James Earl Ray was eventually traced to London, where he was travelling under a false identity. He was arrested at Heathrow Airport and charged with possessing a loaded firearm and false passport. On 10 March 1969 Ray was sentenced to 99 years in jail for the shooting of King. Three days into his sentence Ray recanted his guilty plea and spent the next 29 years fighting for a retrial; he died in jail on 23 April 1998.

Below: **NOTTINGHAM** Heading for Sandiacre, 7 miles west of Nottingham, on 20 August 1968 is Barton No 776 (YNN 776), an Alexander-bodied AEC Reliance new in 1958. *Author's collection*

At approximately 11pm on this day Eastern Bloc armies from four Warsaw Pact countries – the Soviet Union, Bulgaria, Poland and Hungary – invaded Czechoslovakia with 200,000 troops and 2,000 tanks. Romania did not take part in the invasion, nor did Albania, which withdrew from the Warsaw Pact over the matter. Participation of the German Democratic Republic (East Germany) was cancelled just hours before the invasion.

Above: **NOTTINGHAM** In 1961 Mansfield & District acquired four new ECW-bodied Bristol FS6Gs, Nos 531 to 534 (567 to 570 ERR). In early 1968 No 534 was acquired by Midland General, and is seen under new management in Underwood, north-west of Nottingham, on 12 May 1968.

'There has never been a year like 1968, and it is unlikely there will ever be again,' wrote Mark Kurlansky in his book **1968: The Year That Rocked the World.** *'At a time when nations and cultures were still very different, there occurred a spontaneous combustion of rebellious spirits around the world. These protests were not planned in advance, nor did the protesters share an ideology or goal. The one cause many had in common was opposition to America's war in Vietnam, but they were driven above all by a youthful desire to rebel against all that was outmoded, rigid and authoritarian.'*

On 5 June 1968 Robert F. Kennedy was shot at the Ambassador Hotel in Los Angeles, and died from his injuries the next day.

WALSALL During July 1950, No RTL 550 (KYY 643), a Park Royal-bodied Leyland PD/1, entered service with London Transport from Camberwell Depot working routes 36 and 40. After overhaul in March 1954, No 550 was transferred to Stockwell Depot. In December 1957 it was overhauled again at Aldenham, and was then transferred to Chalk Farm Depot where, after a short period of service, it was stored. In August 1959 Walsall Corporation acquired five RTLs, one of which was No RTL 550, and all entered service in September 1959. KYY 643 is seen here at Walsall bus station on 5 June 1968, now numbered 201; it passed to the West Midlands Passenger Transport Executive on 1 October 1969 until September 1971.

WALSALL Also standing in the bus station on the same day is No 124 (ODH 82), a Park Royal-bodied Leyland PD2/1; new in January 1951, it had its bodywork extensively rehabilitated by Metro-Cammell in early 1961. No 124 was transferred to the WMPTE on 1 October 1969, but was very rarely used and was sold for scrap in March 1972. During the Walsall trolleybus era, the Corporation operated a total of nine routes covering 18.86 miles with a maximum fleet of 69. Three months before this view was taken, on 10 March, all Sunday operating of trolleybuses in the Walsall area ceased.

READING This is Reading No 174 (ERD 145), a Park Royal-bodied Sunbeam S7 that entered service on 1 November 1950. It is seen here on 3 February 1968, and just nine months later, on 3 November 1968, trolleybuses in Reading ran for the last time. No 174 is now in preservation.

On this day Richard Nixon, a Republican from California, declared his presidential candidacy. In November 1968 500,000 people marched for peace in Washington, DC, which became the largest anti-war rally in US history.

READING This is No 170 (ERD 141), another Park Royal-bodied Sunbeam S7 that entered service on 1 November 1950 and was withdrawn on 2 November 1968. The photograph is dated 16 May 1968. *Author's collection*

On this day the Ronan Point tower block in Newham, East London, partially collapsed after a gas explosion, killing four occupants.

READING On 1 November and 1 December 1950 12 all-Crossley DD42/8s entered service with Reading Corporation, numbered 84 to 95 (ERD 153 to 164). Nearing the end of their working lives, this view of the rears of Nos 95 and 93 was taken on 3 February 1968 at Mill Lane Depot.

READING Looking across the River Kennet to the back of Mill Lane Depot on the same day, in view is No 3 (MRD 146), a Park Royal-bodied AEC Regent III that entered service on 1 January 1957 and remained in the fleet until 8 November 1987; it has since been preserved. Standing beyond it is No 91 (ERD 160), an all-Crossley DD42/8 that was retired on 26 September 1968.

1968 Happenings (1)

January
Ford Escort car is introduced to replace the Anglia
Cecil Day-Lewis becomes new Poet Laureate
Gardeners' World debuts on BBC1 television, with Percy Thrower

February
Some 1,500 Asians have now arrived in Britain from Kenya, forced out by draconian immigration laws
Northampton is designated a New Town, with the Wilson Government hoping to double its size and population by 1980

March
First performance of an Lloyd Webber/Rice musical, when *Joseph and his Amazing Technicolor Dreamcoat* in its original form is performed by pupils of a school in Hammersmith
Coal mining in the Black Country ends after some 300 years
Demonstration in Grosvenor Square, London, against Vietnam War – 91 police injured, 200 demonstrators arrested

April
London Bridge is sold to an American entrepreneur to be rebuilt at Lake Havasu City, Arizona
Enoch Powell makes his controversial 'rivers of blood' speech on immigration
5p and 10p coins introduced in the run-up to 1971's decimalisation

READING In late 1967 and 1968 Reading Corporation switched its purchasing favours to the Bristol RELL, taking no fewer than 42 to replace the trolleybuses. The first batch had Strachan bodywork, while later purchases had Pennine bodywork to a very similar appearance with space for 35 standing passengers. The REs were very unpopular with the travelling public. This is No 260 (KRD 260F), a Strachan-bodied Bristol RELL, photographed on 3 February 1968; it had entered service on 14 December 1967 and remained with the fleet until 31 December 1982. In the background is No 44 (ADP 944B), an East Lancashire-bodied Dennis Loline III that entered service on 1 July 1964.

In this year the British Post Office introduced First Class post, and since 1968 the number of letters the Post Office delivers has almost tripled from 30 million to 82 million.

Left: **BRISTOL** This is Bristol Omnibus No LC6016 (715 JHY), an ECW-bodied Bristol FSF6B that was new in November 1960. It is seen at Temple Meads railway station on 3 February 1968 working route 17 between the station and the Zoo. Until 1968 British Rail used a rigid price formula for ticket prices – in 1968 it was 3¼d per mile.

Below: **BRISTOL** During October 1965 Bristol's No 2628 (DHW 994C), an ECW-bodied Bristol MW5G, entered service. In September 1967 it was repainted into a livery of cream with green window surrounds and skirting for Bristol's 'City Centre Circle' service, and it is seen in that livery at Temple Meads station on the same day as the previous photograph. This bus would remain in the fleet until sold for scrap in November 1979.

1968 Happenings (2)

May
Ronnie and Reggie Kray are among 18 men arrested in dawn raids, accused of murder, fraud, blackmail and assault
General Assembly of the Church of Scotland permits ordination of women as ministers

June
National Health Service reintroduces prescription charges

July
Alec Rose returns from a 354-day single-handed round-the-world trip and is knighted
Beatles animated film *Yellow Submarine* premiered in London

August
Frigate HMS *Scylla* is final ship built and launched at Devonport's Royal Dockyard
British Rail runs its final standard-gauge steam-hauled train, the famous 'Fifteen Guinea Special'

September
First local authorities adopt three-tier education system, with infant and junior schools replaced by first schools, middle schools and grammar or secondary modern schools
Japanese car-maker Nissan begins importing its range of Datsun cars to Britain
Theatres Act 1968 ends censorship of the theatre, and controversial US musical *Hair* opens in London as a result

MONMOUTH Leaving the town's bus station for Chepstow on 24 June 1968 is Red & White's No U1157 (SAX 987), an ECW-bodied Bristol MW6G new in 1957. *Author's collection*

A new band called the New Yardbirds (successor to the Yardbirds, who had split up in the middle of 1968) began their first tour of the UK on 4 October. On 25 October they played their first show at the University of Surrey, as Led Zeppelin.

Opposite: **CARDIFF** Red & White took delivery of 11 Bristol RELL6Gs in 1965 and gave them a new prefix of 'R' in the fleet number series; the '6G' suffix denoted a Gardner engine. They were used to replace double-deckers on the Cardiff to Gloucester route. Production of the Series 2 version of the RELL with an 18ft 6in wheelbase began in 1967, and Red & White took delivery of five with the Leyland O.600 engine (RELL6L) and dual-purpose 50-seat ECW bodywork. These vehicles had the new standard ECW bodywork for Series 2 REs with a modified front end incorporating a peaked roof dome and a flat windscreen. In 1968 a further 20 RELL6Ls with Leyland O.600 engines were delivered, this time with ECW B53F bodywork of similar external outline to the 1967 deliveries. At Cardiff bus station on 4 February 1968, working the slow service 300 to Bristol via Chepstow, is No R467 (LAX 125F), one of the ECW-bodied Bristol RELL6Ls new in 1967.

Above: **CARDIFF** The city's system was a medium-sized one, with a total of 14 routes and a maximum fleet of 79 trolleybuses. Working route 3 on a wet 4 February 1968 is No 228 (DUH 723), an East Lancashire-bodied BUT 9641T new in 1948. Trolleybus operations on this route would cease in April, and No 228 was withdrawn the following year.

On this day the cult series The Prisoner starring Patrick McGoohan finished its first run on British television.

Right: **CARDIFF** In February 1968 the limited stop service between Cardiff and Bristol was usually operated by Bristol RELLs, and seeing a bus-bodied vehicle on this route was very unusual. Just arrived at Cardiff bus station on 4 February is Red & White's No U2454 (MAX 124), an ECW-bodied Bristol LS6G that entered service in October 1954. In July 1968 No U2454 was sold to Crosville and was allocated the fleet number SUG 291; it was withdrawn in April 1973.

CARDIFF Standing in the bus station on 1 September 1968 is Caerphilly No 23 (YNY 923), one of two Massey-bodied Leyland PD2/40s new in 1958. *Author's collection*

The Bee Gees' I've Gotta Get a Message to You was No 1 in the charts this week.

NEWPORT Standing in Upper Dock Street bus station on 26 February 1968 working route 3A from the town centre to Malpas Road and Brynglas Estate is No 58 (SDW 134), a Longwell Green-bodied Leyland PD2/40 new in 1959. It was sold for scrap in October 1972. *Author's collection*

The No 1 UK single at this time was Mighty Quinn by Manfred Mann, and Diana Ross and the Supremes topped the LP charts with their Greatest Hits.

Photo	DESTINATIONS
67	**TORQUAY**
68	**TORQUAY**
69	**TORQUAY**
70	**TORQUAY**
71	**BOURNEMOUTH**
72	**BOURNEMOUTH**
73	**SANDWICH**

TORQUAY Standing empty in the town on 18 June 1968 is Grey Cars (Devon General) No 3 (3 RDV), a Harrington-bodied AEC Reliance new in April 1964. The entire Grey Cars fleet passed to Greenslades in May 1971; 3 RDV was repainted to white and ivy green livery in 1972, and a year later was repainted again in National Coach livery. In July 1975 the coach passed to Sherris of Carhampton, and three years later to Prestwood Travel, which retained it until September 1984.

On this day Frederick West, Britain's first heart transplant patient, died, 46 days after his operation.

TORQUAY Leaving the resort for Southampton on 17 June 1968 is Grey Cars (Devon General) No 27 (EOD 27D), another Harrington-bodied AEC Reliance, new in April 1966. As with No 3, it passed to Greenslades in May 1971, then was sold to Sykes of Barnsley in December 1975. In February 1976 it was purchased by Davies of Tredegar, and a year later by Stonnis of Tredegar, then, through Baker of Weston-super-Mare, it passed to Wilkins Coaches of Cymmer in September 1977, remaining there until scrapped in March 1983.

In Los Angeles in June of this year the band Iron Butterfly release the album In-A-Gadda-Da-Vida, considered to be one of the earliest examples of the emerging rock genre of 'heavy metal'. The title song was 17 minutes long, but sadly was edited down for release as a single.

TORQUAY On 17 June 1968 we see Devon General No 775 (ROD 775), a Metro-Cammell-bodied AEC Regent V that entered service on 1 January 1956 on Exeter local routes.

A few days earlier women sewing-machinists started a strike at Ford's Dagenham assembly plant for pay comparable to that of men.

TORQUAY Between July and August 1959 Devon General took delivery of 17 Metro-Cammell-bodied Leyland PDR1/1s, Nos DL872 to DL888 (872 to 888 ATA). This is one from that batch, No 875 (875 ATA), working the regular route 12 to from Brixham to Newton Abbot via Torquay and Paignton. The bus had a low-bridge accident and the top deck was rebuilt by Willowbrook.

BOURNEMOUTH In November 1957 two ECW-bodied Bristol LD6Gs entered service with Wilts & Dorset, numbered 630 and 631 (PMR 913 and 914). They made their appearance on the Salisbury to Southampton route apparently in reply to the electrification of the railway between the two places by British Railways a couple of months earlier. This is No 631 looking smartly turned out and working route 38 on 15 July 1968. From 1 October 1972 the Hants & Dorset and Wilts & Dorset fleets were fully merged, and the Wilts & Dorset fleet name was no longer used. On 1 October 1972 both buses passed to Hants & Dorset and No 631 eventually succumbed to National Bus Company livery in January 1974. Brickwoods was a brewery that rose to prominence in the early half of the 20th century after it acquired dozens of breweries across the South East. It was taken over by Whitbread in 1971 and bottling ceased to function at its base in Portsea, Portsmouth, ten years later. The brewery closed for good in 1983, and brewing was transferred to Cheltenham. *Author's collection*

BOURNEMOUTH

No 852 (MLJ 147), an ECW-bodied Bristol LS6G, was one of the first underfloor-engine buses in the Hants & Dorset fleet. The bodywork was of integral construction incorporating cove windows fitted above the main windows and reclining seats. No 852 entered service on 1 May 1953, then in November 1965 was converted to one-person operation by Strachan; the conversion work also included the removal of the headrests and the chrome wheel discs. In October 1967 No 852 was repainted in the dual-purpose livery of green below the waist-rail and cream above. Looking rather tired and bruised in the dual-purpose livery, this view of No 852 was taken on 31 August 1968. *Author's collection*

On the same day the first Isle of Wight Festival began.

SANDWICH At its height pharmaceutical company Pfizer Ltd employed more than 3,000 people at its Discovery Park research and development centre in Sandwich. At Pfizer's on 25 August 1968 is East Kent's FFN 379, a Park Royal-bodied Guy Arab III new in 1951. This bus became a driver trainer in 1974, remaining in that role until April 1977. *Author's collection*

1968
Arrivals & Departures

Arrivals

Heather Mills	Model	12 January
LL Cool J	Rapper/actor	14 January
Lisa Marie Presley	Daughter of Elvis	1 February
Daniel Craig	Actor	2 March
Patsy Kensit	Actress	4 March
Mike Atherton	Cricketer	23 March
Nasser Hussain	Cricketer	28 March
Celine Dion	Singer	30 March
Al Murray	Comedian	10 May
Catherine Tate	Comedian	12 May
Rebekah Brooks	Newspaper journalist/editor	27 May
Kylie Minogue	Singer	28 May
Jason Donovan	Singer/actor	1 June
Jon Culshaw	Impressionist	2 June
Adam Woodyatt	Actor (*EastEnders*)	28 June
Colin McRae	Rally driver	5 August (d. 2007)
Chris Boardman	Cyclist	6 August
Gillian Anderson	Actress	9 August
Julia Sawalha	Actress	9 September
Guy Ritchie	Film director	10 September
Will Smith	Singer/actor	25 September
Mika Hakkinen	Racing driver	28 September

Luke and Matt Goss	Twin singers (Bros)	29 September
Jana Novotna	Tennis player	2 October
Hugh Jackman	Actor	12 October
Ziggy Marley	singer	17 October
Michael Stich	Tennis player	18 October
Owen Wilson	Actor	18 November
Kirsty Young	TV journalist	23 November
Kate Humble	TV presenter	12 December

Departures

Donald Wolfit	Actor-manager	(b1902)	17 February
Yuri Gagarin	Astronaut	(b1934)	27 March
Jim Clark	Racing driver	(b1936)	7 April
Frankie Lymon	Pop singer	(b1942)	30 April
W. E. Johns	Author ('Biggles')	(b1893)	21 June
Tony Hancock	Comedian	(b1924)	24 June
Bud Flanagan	Comedian/singer	(b1896)	20 October
Mervyn Peake	Author/illustrator	(b1911)	17 November
Upton Sinclair	Author	(b1878)	25 November
Enid Blyton	Children's author	(b1897)	28 November
John Steinbeck	Author	(b1902)	20 December

1968
Happenings (3)

October
First recorded instance of live sextuplets in UK are born in Birmingham

British racing drivers Jackie Stewart, Graham Hill and John Surtees take first three places at US Grand Prix

Olympic Games held in Mexico City

National Giro opens for business through the GPO

Alan Bennett's play *Forty Years On* premieres in London

November
Cyril Lord carpet business goes into receivership

Race Relations Act makes it illegal to refuse housing, employment or public services to people because of their ethnic background

Government extends boundaries of Dawley New Town in Shropshire and renames it Telford

Trade Descriptions Act prevents misleading product descriptions by shops and traders

December
Official opening of first phase of Royal Mint's new Llantrisant plant in South Wales

Contemporary vehicles 1968

SOUTHAMPTON DOCKS How many car makes and models can you spot? This view illustrates a wealth of contemporary vehicles that were on our roads back in 1968. Surprisingly there is not a bus in sight or is there? Buses come in many sizes and by way of example, the early Ford Transit with its two rear doors open could perhaps be deemed a minibus. . *Silver Link Archive/Ray Ruffell Collection*

Index of Operators and Vehicles